Growing Pains
&
Grass Stains

By RJ Wright

310 BROWN STREET

Edited By: Sunni Soper
& Christopher Michael

Released December *2017*

Published by:

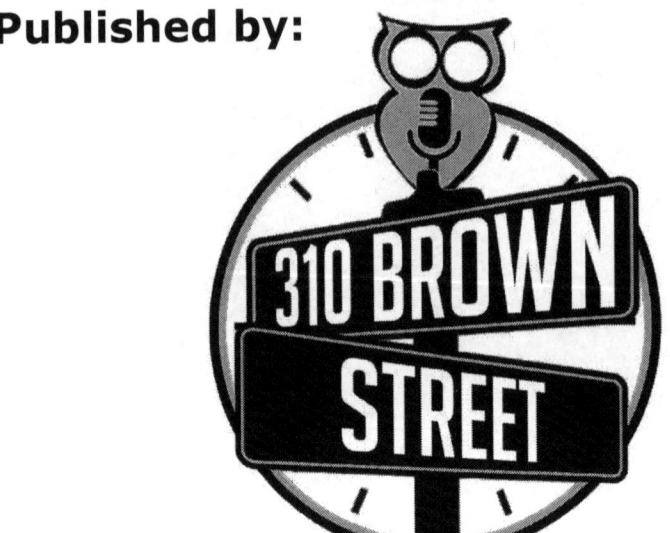

Printed in the United States of America
ISBN 978-0-9984270-8-9
Published by 310 Brown Street
www.310brownstreet.com
book.rj.wright89@gmail.com

Table of Contents

Grass Stains

Pains

Growing

Grass Stains

Open Prayer to God I

I want to be bigger God
I want to be the best at everything I try, so I try everything
Tyron say this makes me greedy
Say I should just sit down somewhere

In church, they said, "we are born into sin"
I'm not sure how. I don't understand how just being, is a sin.
How being born makes me unworthy of your love

In church, they say come to God as though you are a child
I'm not sure what they mean because I'm only six

I like church God
Especially when they let me take pieces of you home in my pockets
Especially when they let me play the drums
When they let me be the rhythm everything moves to

I love you God. Even when things don't go my way
Mom say I should praise you
Should give you the glory and you will turn it around

But I pray every night and I can't tell if anything is turning or
changing, but...

I pray
I pray
I pray
I pray because when you're a child God is the only one who
listens

Mom

When asked if I ever write about happy things
I grin then reply
Rarely
Only when I'm writing about her
She is a light house
Kept me from shipwrecking in the dark
My mother is the kind of woman who helps you shoulder your burdens before you can see them
The kind of woman who folds her own into slips of paper and places them in a Bible
A metaphor for how you can solve any problem if you surround it with the word of God
The kind of woman who handles a switch like she is conducting an orchestra
Always keeping us on key and in tune
My mother is the kind of woman who loves her sons with her words and her hands
Held us the way tears hold sorrow and joy simultaneously
Like only a mother knows how
I don't often remember crying, but if I did, it was probably because she did first
And she did, a lot!
But always followed it with a smile like a rainbow after a storm
That reminded us, that should never leave us
My mother is her own kind of gospel, every breath a hymn
I left the house at eighteen, but I took her melody with me
When my apartment feels more holding area than home
I play her voicemails as if they were my favorite song
So yeah, I write about the happy
It's called Mom

Family

My family is its
Own kind of battlefield, we
Embrace endless love

My family is its
Own kind of loving embrace
We fight endlessly

My family is it
It is all love and fight, and
Happy pains, that's family

Shedding Skins

I've had several names in my life, each a skin with a different
shade and texture
They shed in just the same manner they were formed
Each layer of armor growing below the last

My mother, but mostly father, named me Robert
Named after my grandfather
A hand-me-down from a generation I knew little about

But this name be a promise that I'm connected to something
other than myself
In school, I was called:
                    Captain America
                    Foreign
                    Stupid
                    Dyslexic
                    But I answered to RJ

A name of my own design
Radically Justified in its creation
In my need to define myself
In college, they called me England
It seemed I had a British flag for a tongue

And they could hear it waving every time I would ask a
question.
My presence was an awkward statement

Like a rhetorical question punctuated by an exclamation point
No one knew how to respond to me
So, I went unanswered

Each name lightning, bottled in this tinted glass frame
A bright frame

It's funny how I can tell when and how well people know me
based on the name they call

Gaps

I hate smiling. Let one more person tell me to smile,
There's gone be some consequences and repercussions
That require a concussion protocol

There are missing moments in my grin
So, stop asking me to smile
Just reminds me of all the sleep I lost over gap jokes

A few ex-girlfriends ago this woman who didn't belong to me said:
"The space in between my teeth contains the void God used to form
the heavens and earth with"

I didn't realize my teeth had enough space between them to fit a Big
Bang . . .but ok, thanks... I think

I think she thought this was a compliment
I felt like an eight-year-old getting a sweater for Christmas
I wouldn't appreciate this until I got older

No one has ever fallen in love with my smile
Nor complimented me on its lack of completeness

They fall in like with my mine field of a mouth
And the tongue inhabiting it

Sometimes when flossing or brushing, I find things

Things that don't belong, like shoe leather and shovels
from conversations where I couldn't find the right... the right... the
right...
My mind is always biting off more than my mouth can communicate

WORDS! I can never find the right words!

My top and bottom teeth have always had an uneasy truce

You can see it in the way they come together in an awkward hand shake

I used to look gift horses in the mouth
But I'm a quick learner
Shoot even my momma will tell you

I learned to speak patriarchy before I could piece together the syllables of my own name
So, forgive me when I default to it
I'm still learning to Rosetta Stone it out of my lexicon

Ain't that privilege?
To apologize for something
That at some point I know I will do again

Or maybe it's just the Christian in me
Always looking for forgiveness and haven't finished repenting

No this is not an ally poem
Just a filling for the cavity in my ego

I hate this breath of mine, some days it smells
Like an attack dog on a summer day in Selma

But I love this voice
This voice, it don't do vulnerable well
But it can swing anger like a billy club on a black body

Ferociously and with no care about who's watching
Stop telling me to smile
Just reminds me of all the times I've been left bloodied by my own reflection

Normally I'm the gap where insecurities go to hide, but lately
I stuff as much fly boy and black magic under my tongue as I can
In order to origami these words into confidence
And crash into the holes on the side of your face

I'm indifferent about my lips, they are full
yet seemingly awkwardly shaped.
My mouth is always in search of something holier
than itself to embrace.

Home

The only problem with having a designated function
Is that most times what you were created to do is the only way people see you
I'm no different, most days I'm a hospital waiting room
A place no one wants to be
A place where everyone coronates their terror
Their pain
And on rare occasions, relief that they're leaving my presence without need of repair
Nerves are rubbed raw waiting for a conclusion we are all afraid to face
Far too often death finds its home in me, and my poetry
If these rib caged walls could talk
They would speak of how good and bad news caress the same on the faces of the weary and rest
With tears blooming slowly, then erupt all at once
In a past life, I think I was an attic, another place where ghosts dwell
They are so comfortable filling the empty spaces people have left in me
In my next life, I want to be a bedroom a place where life is sown
Instead of reaped
A place where reapers don't wander so freely
A shelter from the uncertainty that haunts my vacant
Most people think themselves a house with many corridors and chambers
But I would settle for being a room in someplace more home than hospice
A place I can feel a part of something bigger than myself
Every day I attempt to make myself a welcoming space
I'm still waiting for someone to call me home

In Dyslexia

You, know who irritates me from the very trenches of my soul
Grammar Nazis
You know the people
Who in the abstinence
I MEAN absence of an intelligent argument will stifle,
I MEAN sniper EVERY, SINGLE, MISSPELLING

Or missing capital letters after a period
Two words convict clues
I MEAN CONTEXT CLUES.
Words are really hard

> Ask any 3-year-old... or Donald Trump
> I relate a lot to 3-year-olds
> The first girl I ever wrote a love letter to
> Responded by saying "you write like a toddler"

She laughed as she read every spelling and grammar mistake
In front of a cackling chorus of schoolgirls
Since that day, I haven't been able to un-write the reflection
I MEAN rejection

I MEAN I have **dyslexia**
A disorder that involves being ridiculed
I MEAN difficulty reading and writing

> And the way you're looking right now
> Is the reason I hate telling people
> Because you look at me like a paragraph
> Without punctuation maybe you could understand me
> If you took the time

School was an exercise in ridicule
I MEAN repetition
Teacher would rather throw me a ball than help me understand a book
Felt like being trained to sit to roll over to good dog

Teachers saw me as the runt of the litter
I was the student they seldom called on

But my classmates never stopped calling

They call me slow!   short bus! Stpiud!
stupid

I hate feeling

So, I learned to be a crown cast
I MAEN class clown
To make myself a joke before others could
But sometimes the laughter sounds like sit, like roll over, like bad dog,

Like you're still stupid

It makes me want to chew on the throats of people
Who invalidated my existence because I used the wrong your or you're

But I'm black
So, I can't give America an excuse to put me down
What is being black in America
If not an exercise in editing one's self

                    To be dyslexic is to be a grown man
                    Who is still afraid to read out loud?
                    It is to see the read
                    I MEAN red and green lines below your words as
                    wounds
                    You can bandage with spell check

It is to call autocorrect Judas
But know your mind is the betrayer
My mind plays tricks on me
I can read my Facebook status 500 times

And still not to my catch error
I MEAN erred to my not catched

17

I MEAN I need to make the words stop

Crashingintooneanother

Feels
        like I'm reading

   in an **earthquake**

           where nothing sits still

   long enough to make snese

What do you do when
Every classroom still feels like an

 ?

Where I relive stumbling through *Of Mice and Men*
In front of a jury of my adolescent tears
I MEAN peers

I mean THE BEST teachers
Are people who love you
School never made me feel worthy of love
So, my mother turned her embrace into a classroom

She would tell me
"You are gifted"
"You are blessed"
"You are fearfully and wonderfully made"
"You are a success story in the making"
"Your mind is anointed"

                    I know I

        am!

But most days
My mind still feels like a
beautiful curse
the ugliest of blessings

My mom reminds me
"regardless of what your mind is, it is yours
So, speak life into it"

But speaking life has never been my issue
It is reading and writing it that scares me.

Love

At first, I couldn't tell whether....
Nope that's not the proper way to intro this story

Ok, fresh tactics
Has anyone else ever joined a cult by accident?...

No... just no, just me?
Ok, hear me out.
I now understand how someone
becomes a trump supporter

I've been told it's the same as "falling in love is like falling
asleep, happens slowly then all at once"

At least that's what the girl from the fault in our starts said
And I watched the fault in our start, so I think I understand
love
'Cause I used to write a lot of love poems

Like an obscene amount of gushy
you are my queen, I want to be your king kinda shit

Yeah, I stopped.

Somewhere in the midst of racism
Situation-ships and not knowing
If what I was writing reinforced
The systemic oppression of women, I got confused

Overlooked love's ability to crown those
Who subjugate themselves to it
Letting go and letting love
Has never been something I received a passing grade in

Learned happily ever after is for kids and fairy tales
Further proof that growing up, is in fact, a trap

In my spare time, I rewrite the endings to romantic comedies
To make them more realistic
You know, my life is basically romantic comedy...
Without the Hollywood ending...
Or romance...
Or comedy...

Ok, maybe I need a new metaphor
'Cause love kinda sucks
Ok, correction, love doesn't suck, people do

People love to talk about falling
But never have any answers for
What happens when you hit the ground

And I know some of you are thinking
What does love have to do with being in a cult?
Or being a trump supporter?
And I'm getting there

So, love has a way of grabbing you without your permission

Of thinking it can enter your space without waiting for your consent
Of convincing you that it can fix all the problems

That if necessary, it will build walls to protect you
From those who would do you harm, even if no one is doing you harm
Has a way of making you feel like the world will end without it

Like everything that came before it was horrible in comparison
And that it is going to be fantastic, believe me it is
Just fantastic

It makes you feel valued and heard
Even if your ideals are hateful and a little racist

Ok, so I'm not saying I agree
Just that I kinda under... nope, still don't get it

Wow, this really is just like love, confusing and full of WTFs
Ok, no, I don't think I explained this well
Let me try a different approach

So, love is...

Pains

Open Prayer to God II

Holy Spirit, I wanted to pray to you, specifically
Seems like, of the trinity, people leave you out
Or forget about you and I can relate

You are the diary where I keep all my secrets.
I'm afraid someone might read this and think me
Reducing you to words in-between the pages of a book
Written with human hand. Because who would be
stupid enough to do that?

It's a lot easier not to sin when you don't know what sinning is...
Or at least it feels that way

I'm not saying ignorance and innocence are the same.
I am saying that both kiss my mouth with naive lips
And absent-minded tongue

I think most days, I'm just happy to be kissed.

Black Face

White girl, paints face black; captions photo
"When your trying to fit in at your HBCU"
A friend points out this would be funny had she not been in black
face
And I laugh as I think it's funny how the masks we choose expose us
About how she uses the word "your" to take ownership of something
she has no desire to be a part of
Historically Black Colleges and Universities
Have in truth been the only place we felt conquer felt nourished felt
swan instead of ugly duckling
Misfit is a shape we have been concubine to since whiteness became
synonymous with supremacy
She has yet to be expelled and if she is not
I won't be able to help but blame
The A&M noosing our purple and gold hymns of praise
Ain't that privilege?
That your willful ignorance can make you into a rallying cry
Helen of Troy reincarnated, the face that launched a thousand
retweets
This ain't no burning cross
It's that nagging back injury
That reminds you of your limited range of motion every time you try
to stretch your boundaries
At Prairie View A&M University, we don't walk on the grass because
we know not what patches of earth be graves
We wonder if every tree be a Christmas tree once ornamented by
black bodies that swayed with the caroling of clansmen
This hill used to feel love a pride confessing
Now it just feels like a cliff we are being pushed off of
It's hard to be productive when you have nowhere to call home
Ain't got nowhere we call sanctuary, outside of our own bodies
Is there anywhere left we are allowed feel whole?

Popcorn

I love food
I hold this truth to be self-evident
At 6 years old, POPCORN was my favorite snack
ready to eat in 2 minutes or less
Because at 6, any longer is an eternity

It always POPPED in the space between meals
Comfort for cuts and bruises, a well done for a perfect POP quiz
It's always been and indicator that something was going to happen
These days there is no short of happening

At 6 years old, my spine straightened just long enough
During a traffic stop to tell a police officer
Exactly what little black boys think of him
Strangling a bag of Orville Redenbacher
I said, "Mr. Officer, are you going to shoot us?"

I watched his face fold in to itself
As he realized what it felt like to have his voice box hand cuffed
I can't write fast enough to keep up with the popping.
Black bodies are popped in 2 seconds or less
Any longer would feel like an eternity

Never enough time to sit on your stomach
Instead we throw-up
Half-digested cellphone video
On every social media platform available
Hoping we can fat shame the chefs
Serving us readymade mistreatment
Melted over
Mal-nutritious
Murder manifested as

Mere misfortune and
Misunderstanding.
I wish these shots wouldn't POP the spot so often

The confederacy may have gone the way of the dinosaurs
But discrimination doesn't burn as easily
As confederate flags or POPCORN
Jim Crow didn't die, he just revamped the menu

Tonight, we are serving negro skinned n sautéed
Over a bed of blackened badges and flamed crosses
Eh, waiter there was a mistake

I ordered a conviction
With a throw him under the jail house salad.
But you brought me a
Failure to indict with a side of he had it coming

Left wondering if justice tastes sweet or savory
So, when someone shoots a cop
I cry even though it's just desserts.

Tired of plating benefit of doubt
Devouring innocent until proven guilty
When the same burden of proof never stomach aches
The blue lives that matter so much

Black bodies don't hang from trees any more
They slow cook in project crock pots
'Til freedom falls off the bone
Ready to eat as soon as these braised bullets POP
The life out of them
No wait, I forgot about Atlanta and Mississippi
Niggas are still hanging from trees

Be gluttonous

Eat 'til you burst at the entrance wound
I mean exit wound
I mean the noose
I mean seams

Eat whatever you want as long as there is no nutritional value
Your diet should consist of sweet tea, skittles
You know, movie theatre food

Food that indicates something is about to happen
These days there is no shortage of happening

Can you smell the...
Can you hear the POP...
          POP   POP
POP
                POP   POP
POP
                POP

Can you feel your mouth watering?
The way it does before you vomit
I wonder when America will be ready
For a new favorite snack

Tug of War

Every day she does a balancing act
She walks a fine line in the midst of a war zone

And what a walk it is.
A mixture of a John Coltrane solo
and a Fort Worth skyline just boxing
with a lightning storm

Sunrise smile painted from ear to ear
while trying not to get caught in the cross fire
between her heart and her head

She has been searching for a middle ground for a while now.
For somewhere she can escape the sound
of her war-torn heart's battle cries
for a genuine love from a genuine lover

A place where her fear of being loved won't wear strength
as a Halloween costume and attempt to
destroy anything that gets too close

She can't seem to escape the tug of war between
her heart and her head

I've seen how this battle plays out,
more often than not, in the case of the unstoppable force
meets the immovable object
the head won't allow the heart to move it

But regardless of the mass casualties and the death toll
THERE IS SOMETHING, about the way she pirouettes
through the minefield of mistrust,
heartbreak and hope that makes
me want to take a flying leap into her arms

When I know what I want, I have a tendency to
throw myself head-first into the eye of the storm
whether it is a drizzle or a downpour

But we didn't come here to talk about me.
We are here because this song bird woman
with a symphony of phoenix wings for legs
a shotgun for a mouth
and Excalibur tongue that
cuts and slashes through men unworthy
of her company

Yet wears the weight of her dead relationships like camouflage
you can't quite see it, but you know there's something there.
I can see her second guessing herself with my eyes closed

If I could write her ex a letter, I would read dear boy dear mister
excuses
I want to thank you for making the mistake of mistreating God's
gift to Adam

I want to thank you for taking her to the breaking point so now
she will appreciate the way I hold her together when I wrap my
arms around her

Dear ex-lover of my future wife
I want to thank you for mistreating God's gift to Adam
I want to thank you for never fucking her properly
I want to thank you for giving her a first-class education
in ain't shit niggas

I want to thank you for taking her to
her breaking point so she can appreciate
the way my embrace glues her back together

But that is only if she lowers her defenses

long enough for these unholy hands to wipe away
her tears and quiet her cries
I wish my voice was as comforting to her as a woodwind chorus'
melody

But this isn't about me
It's about a woman who's stranded in
no man's land being pulled apart by
rival ends of an emotional spectrum
not knowing whether she wants to truly
strive for love or stay comfortably
disappointed

I just know she deserves a happily ever after
One where her husband makes love to her
like the sun is about to fall from the sky
I don't get to decide the ending to this story

But I hope the first step begins with her lips
meeting my lips on the corner of desire boulevard
and insatiable avenue until we are breathless
and weightless floating suspended
above everything that keeps us earth bound

But again, this isn't about me.
I am not the architect in-charge of
constructing the ever after to this fairy tale
but I hope she designs a future
that includes my presence

Never Made It

"I have never been to New Orleans;
I wanna go someday, maybe next year"

Our last conversation wasn't one of consequence
Mostly bullshit and bravado
I can't help thinking to myself
On your last day on earth, did anyone make you feel
Loved?

Did you tell your mother what she meant to you?
I imagine you painting a smile on her face, supernova bright
And now I'm sure she feels like she's living in the shadow of a
solar eclipse.
No parent should have to bury their child

Sleep isn't coming as easily as it once did
I'm tossing and turning in these bed sheets until I'm cocooned
They say sleep and death are cousins
But lately they feel more like Siamese twins

Lately they feel more like praying hands
Did you commune God in the moments
Before your eyes closed for the final time?

Did you ask for forgiveness?
Did you praise him for how far he's brought you?
Or did you just ask for restful sleep and tranquil dreams?

But what dream could have been so captivating
That it convinced you to reside in its interior for an eternity?
NO ONE TOLD YOU IT WAS OK TO LEAVE
Why did you leave?

We never know when our last moment will be

So why do we waste time?
"I have never been to New Orleans
I want to go someday, maybe next year"

All my problems seem so insignificant
I realize that there will come a day
When I lie casketed, swallowed by earth in all directions

But before I go sit at my father's feet
I pray I leave a legacy of touched lives
And loved ones just like you have

"I have never been to New Orleans, but
I wanna go someday, maybe next year"

El Choppo, your nickname
Doesn't mean cut or chop
Or barber, but that was Tyler
You made not making sense one of your greatest successes

Whiz kid with clippers and a razor, you had a serrated smile
That could scalpel the crooked and ugly
Out of situations and appearances
'Til their lines were casket sharp

Never in a rush, you realized
When people love you, they will wait on you
So, some part of me must have loved you
Because patience has never been one of my strengths

There were times when I would swear
You were full of shit, and then you would turn
A brawl into barbershop banter in less than a breath

"I have never been to New Orleans
I wanna go someday, maybe next year"

33

Tyler, I will carry your spirit in this poem
I will carry it to every place you never made it to in life
I will spit it in the middle of the French Quarter
Dodging beads and bullets

I keep imagining you in heaven
Giving edge ups to angels and teaching
Your unborn children how to throw a perfect spiral
I pray you are at peace

"I never been to New Orleans
I wanna go someday, maybe next year"

Tyler go ahead and rest, I will make sure you make it to New
Orleans

Questions That Need Answers

Do you know if you were born into the world screaming?

Have you imagined if you will leave in the same fashion?

Will it be loud, boisterous, a celebration of a life lived?

Will it be quiet?

Will there be tearful whispers about grit and determination?

How long have you been in pain like this?

What does it feel like to have your body declare civil war on itself?

When it's over, does your heart get to seek help for the scars we can't see?

How long have you felt hollow?

Or when was the last time you felt whole?

Do you believe yourself?

Did you know that asking questions is a sign of dominance?

Is that why you're always looking for answers instead of asking the question?

How long have you felt like an outsider?

Why are you talking to them?

Do you think they understand you?

What happens when your depression has psychotic features?

Why do they call it hurting yourself?

This is not hurting, it's the ultimate end to all pain?

Do you have a plan?

Do you have access to the means to complete your plan?

Do you think your loved ones will forgive you?

Are you still there?

Answers That Need Questions

My birth was a whisper.

I Pray my life is significant enough that my death rattles the soul of everyone who once called me a lover

It will be a tearful joy, a mournful laughter that asks for solitude, but requires company

They will say he fought, he struggled, he won and lost.

Pain has been a state of mind I could not escape ever since I realized my mind is a landscape no one wanted to explore.

Like all wars, no one wins. No feels the loss more deeply than the battlefield itself, it be home to so many impromptu endings

My heart learned long ago scars are just after-action reviews that teach people how to hurt you better. So it hides them, even from itself.

I don't remember ever feeling full.

When she held me.

I believe in many things that have disappointed me, myself included.

You just called me submissive. That was a stupid question

So far, I haven't asked anything

I answered that question already, why aren't you listening. They never listen. This this why I only talk to you.

I talk to them because they don't ask me stupid questions.

They understand me more than you do.

I don't think I have psychotic features, I just converse with myself sometimes.

I don't know. It doesn't feel like hurting yourself. Sometimes it feels like the only way to feel.

This is not hurting, it's the ultimate end to all pain.

No

I said no

Stop asking me questions.

Random Thoughts

Sometimes people want to be mad. LET THEM! Their mood don't dictate your achievement.

Stop focusing on what you get out of a relationship And focus on what you bring

How can someone be right and so damn wrong at the same time

Note to my future wife: I promise not to leave a trail of clothes from the front door to the bedroom every day

You are worthy

You are loved

You are enough

Things I promise to do in my next relationship:

push you to be great

hold you accountable

tell you no

be affectionate

make you laugh

comfort you

share your burdens

pray for you

pray with you

be affectionate (in public let them watch)

say I love you and not be scared

take care of the people you hold dear

compromise

communication

be vulnerable

be a leader

allow myself to be led

protect you

make eye contact

tell you what I need (be vulnerable)

tell you what you mean to me

You ever walk past someone and they smell like bad decisions and sleepless nights

Sometimes you have to put a condom over your heart and fuck your feelings

Fellas huddle up: there are just some thing you can't say because you're a man. It's the same thing with white people and nigga. Dry them tears and get over it. #getyomans

I high key feel sorry for heterosexual women cause heterosexual poets poets are a raggedy male poets are a raggedy looking bunch

BLACK WOMEN
ARE EVERYTHING
THAT IS ALL.

You can't fix a problem you don't acknowledge

I don't understand everything. That's ok

It Was A Girl

My best friend is the kind of friend who loves you in spite of your flaws. Whose eyes cuss you out before she can part her lips
She is more than a friend, she is family

She is one of the strongest people I know. At 5 feet tall, she has always had a sense of humor that stands like a 300-year-old oak tree in the middle of a field full of driftwood

However today there is no ocean of laughter for us to swim in
Today, she resembles an acorn drowning in a sea of white sheets
For months, we gleefully debated the gender of the magic brewing in her belly

We would laugh so hard, but today she is what I imagine a broken heart looks like, cracked open and bludgeoned, barely beating
She has always been my vault, knows how to wrap her arms around my secrets

But today, she is being looted, emptied of the treasure that called her home
As we, a gallery of onlookers observes how she is

coiled in contractions

I can see her fighting back the tears
I wish I knew how to fight with her
My best friend's voice is an ebbing tide on a sandy
beach

I thought while giving birth, she would tsunami her
voice 'til everything in the room is drenched in pain
and curse words
But this hospital room contained the loudest silence I
had ever heard

It hangs here, thick and humid with a gritty stillness
that makes you desperate to wash it away with a
scream or a song

There is no melody here
Just a stillborn
She still refuses to cry

I want to tell her, you are loved
To give her a safe place to be broken, but I am no
use.
Life proves there is no such thing as a safe space

She has an affinity for camouflaging insecurity into
confidence, pain into laughter. You can't quite see it,

41

but you know it's there
So she makes jokes

Guilty laughter and tearful smiles gingerly tip toe
across my cheeks. I smile to dam the stream pooling
on my face. Her mother uses torso as blanket, tries to
hide my best friend from the world

But my best friend doesn't blame the world
Blames her own body
Calls it betrayer

I want to tell her…. it's not your fault,
You can do everything right and this world will still
take from you
I've seen this world take so much from my best
friend

I want to give it back to her
To hang life by its ankles
Until every piece of joy, it ripped from her falls at
her feet

I want to bully life for her, what good are my hands
if I can't use them to fix the problems of the people I
love…
Fixing is all I know how to do

I couldn't even comfort her
I just watched her rock her premature masterpiece
Back into the arms of God

Finally tears fall
And all I hear is Stevie Wonder's
Isn't She Lovely playing in my head

As I attempt to gather what little courage
I have as an offering, she whispers
"It was a girl. I have been calling her a him for
months now. I hope she forgives me"

Again

It happened again

I watched the strongest human I know do something superhuman again

It was a girl again

She didn't make it again

She was before her time again

She gave her daughter a name again

She looked at her lovingly again

And I wondered if there is a God, why would you do this to her again?

What do you tell a woman when God keeps calling pieces of her back to his throne again and again?

She wouldn't cry again

Fought for every ounce of control again

Her mother held her again

But this time was different and she has the battle scars to prove it

They will serve as reminder that something beautiful once called her home

Once knew her voice without ever seeing her face

There are no tears again

Just dry sadness

Just defiant

Just daring you to think yourself worthy of tears

So, I don't cry again

I sit still again

I wonder what I can give as offering again

And then the strongest human I know says, "I knew it was a girl this time"

And I think how can one person be this strong, again?

Honest and Appropriate

People keep telling me I need to deal with the wrath I have dry docked in my spirit
Cannons aimed at my father's casket

At his funeral, my mother said I want you to speak
She said I want you to be honest and appropriate
But honestly, there has never been anything appropriate about my father
So, I ain't got nothing to say

But if I did, I'd say
I don't know when anger first found a home in me
It's always paid rent on time, so I have never had cause for eviction

The razor bumps on my face are evidence of the fact
You never taught me the building blocks of manhood
Never taught me what it meant to protect a woman, mind and spirit
Blew through their bodies like confetti in a wind tunnel

My EX-girlfriend's voice cracked under the weight of her tears
As she told me I gave you my all
And all you gave me was
Material for my next I hate men poem
She was crying over me, but she was talking to you

By today's standard, you would be a fuck boy
A seller of dreams if you will
It's almost funny
I struggled so hard to not be a salesman
I turned into an honest thief

Instead of auctioning dreams
I abduct visions of the future

Ironically the results are the same

Good women terrify me
I don't know if I'm capable of loving that kind of holy
I fear loving a woman like my mother will make me more you
Then I already am

You taught me what it meant to be man and mouse
simultaneously
Taught me to fear the backbone in my own voice
Ironically the part of you that lingers in my mind
Is the bite in your bark

I didn't cry at your funeral, the anger you taught me
Convinced me that you weren't worth my tears
That I didn't need you

My brothers and I box each other over broken feelings
And bruised promises we never made to each other
We blacken eyes and break ribs jabbing at you
So, if I did have anything to say

I would say:

Who gave your mistress permission to ring me?
I don't care if my father is fastened into his deathbed
I refuse to listen to the sound of her heart breaking at LTE
speeds

Let Tenderness Endure
I can hear my mother's voice rattling around my cranium
But forgiveness doesn't move at version speeds
So, I proceed to dismiss my mother's villain
And my father's toy my, GET OFF MY PHONE, insult her
I wanted to injure you

My father loved us the way his father's absence taught him
Fearful and distant

47

He always coupled the words
I love you with goodbye or talk of his death

Explains why the words I love you
Sound like warning shots telling me the end is coming

My father, whose whereabouts in the afterlife I know not
CAN YOU HEAR ME? I WANNA TELL YOU

Forgiveness is an architect, anger is demolition crew
Forgiveness is graceful, anger is clumsy
Forgiveness is a strength, anger is weakness
If I could talk to you one last time
I would say, "I love you"

But loving you hasn't given me the strength to forgive you yet
Mom, is that that appropriate?

Real News

Today, I woke up to flashes
To the thunder of shudders
To the off-pitch squeal of microphones
To dreams snuffed out by chalk outlines and yellow tape

They are the kind of lovers that show up when we are in pain.

Not to comfort, but to vulture
To pick our bones clean
To nourish themselves with
our destruction, with our yearning
to feel whole and heard

You're never here for our joy because capturing our good never
seems to be newsworthy

Hands

My mother's hands speak love
My father's hands spoke destruction
I'm still learning mother's language

These days, I speak my mother's dialect
With my father's accent translation
destroying everything I love

My mother's hands be adverbs, they
modify everything that comes after them

They turn houses to happy homes
They are the only dwelling that never made me pay rent

My father's hands made me pay for everything, especially my
mistakes

My father's hands be nouns, be persons, places, and things I
run from

But my mother's hands be nouns, too
They be the things I run to
I speak and touch these
It's always been clearer this way
Needs less syntax

10 Things
I Wanna Say to the Girl
I'm Too Afraid to Approach

To the girl who sits in front of me in class
The girl I see every Monday on my way to work
The girl I see every Tuesday and Thursday at the gym
The girl that I see every Wednesday at Starbucks
The girls I see every Friday night at the bar
The girl I see jogging past my house every Saturday morning

1. I'm not stalking you,
but I have been noticing you for a while now
so, in those moments where my gaze seems to linger
a few fractions of a second too long, just realize

I'm trying to construct a sentence
that would let you know I am genuinely interested
in getting to know what rests beneath the beauty in your skin

2. I wonder how long it took God to find
the perfect shade of ebony to wrap your smile in

3. I want to tell you all of this
but so far, I haven't even gathered up enough
courage to say, "Hi"

Too afraid to leave and insignificant impression
or that my compliments might just be seen as an attempt
to see your legs spread across my bed sheets
And I just wanna see an infectious smile spread across your
face

4. I say infectious because when you smile
lights seem to brighten in an attempt to smile back

51

5. I know you have been worn out by
the cat calls, the whistles, the AYO MA's, the YO RED SHIRT
So now you're wearing this expressions that says,
"FUCK YOU, DON'T TALK TO ME," as if it was your favorite
blouse

6. I wanna know your name
See, I know your parents had to search
through eternity's attic to find one
that could match your munificence

So, you don't speak it often, only bartering it
with those who approach you
with more than a modicum of respect.

7. I wanna get to know you
the real you
the stressed out you
the struggling you
the anger management issues you
The 3am and drunk dialing you
the 6am and no makeup you

8. I want to be able to stroll down the corridors
–of your mind so you don't have to tell me
what you're thinking

9. I'm so used to rejection that if you want me to come say hi,
I need a sign

Like wink once
milly rock
moon walk
jump up and down
wave your arms

and then wave me over

cause I'm probably gonna miss all of that

9. When I see you move through a room
you look like a black diamond
Swimming in a sea full of rhinestones

9. I wanna know what your inner thigh tastes like
at sunrise and sunset
so, I can compare and contrast the difference

9. Given the proper time space
and opportunity, I feel like we could fall in love

9. I know I said ten things
but without even speaking
you managed to have me transfixed
so, I can't end this poem
'til I make you feel a fraction of the same.

10. Hello my name is...
Oh, you have a boyfriend...
Ok

Lies We Tell

She had a body like a Friday night
Full of a week's worth of stress, expectation, laughter, and just
the right amount of sin
So, I will make love to her like a Sunday morning worship
service
Loud
Every stroke a song we draw out and crack open into climax
I order my hands along her spine and finger my way to the nape
of her neck
Cradle her head in my palms
She's got a Wednesday for a mind
Always in the center of everything
My hands be adventurers grabbing as many fistfuls of gorgeous
as they can carry
Bury my fingers in her tangled roots and pluck her from the
cotton soil of bed sheets 'til we are face to face
Garden to gardener
She is fertile ground so I plant lips everywhere in need of a
bountiful harvest
I whisper statements in the form of questions
"Let me have you"
And although I know the answer
I wait for her response because consent is the sexiest thing to
fall from a mouth
We have the hungriest of bodies
Tongues that devour each other
Switch blades stitching names into inner thigh, small of back,
center of chest, labia, minora, majora, clitoris
There is no greater union than my tongue pressed to your body
We braid them together like Tuesdays and Thursdays 'til we
reach a weakened end
Make ourselves a Shakespearean creature
Beast with two backs
We are the kind of animal that feeds on itself
Use my body to part hers

She contracts when filled properly
Yet she be Saturday afternoon comfortable enough to sleep in
when my work is through
Nights like these are far from the fairy tales we tell our children
about
They are the legends we remember fondly and drag from our
mind's basement
When our lust is full and our satisfaction is as empty
as Monday morning
We tell ourselves all we need is a night
Knowing full well we are starving for a lifetime

The End

It never starts with secrets,
With angry voices,
With wounded pride,
Or stubborn tears

But it almost always ends that way
I only write poems about things I love
Which is why I couldn't write about myself for the longest

I only write poems about things that cause me pain
Which is why I could only right about myself for the longest

I only write about things I love
Or cause me pain
You do both, so from now on
Everything I write will be about you
And what it means when I say, "I love you."

I love you
Which is to say, I wish we fit together properly

I love you
Which is to say, you have the ability to hurt me the most

I love you
Which is to say, I don't know how to be without you

At night I mold my pillows into the shape of your body
Place my head where your bosom would be
It's the only thing that makes the lonely taste less like forever

My bed isn't mine any more
Your memories acquired it in a hostile take over

When you left they stayed and
Have been auctioning my 2ams to pain and despair ever since
I don't have enough heart to buy them back
Because you took that, too

We broke up in text
Partially because "NOTHING" was ever your fault
Partially because I loved myself just enough
To know you weren't doing it right

But really 'cause you wouldn't even answer my phone calls
You kept sending me to voicemail.
So, I left a voicemail, A VOICEMAIL!
Do you know how angry you have to be to leave a voicemail in
2017?

There was a time when you were the reason for my happy
A time when your smile was my peace
When you would lose your smile
I would always help you dig it out of whatever grave you left it
in

But when we exhumed your smile
And my peace never returned, you never questioned it.

Before you, I had a few relationships,
They were like the 4th of July, full of noise and fireworks
But I never thought you would burst so
Brightly at the chance to be independent of me

Or maybe we have been dying since I said,
"Hello"

The beginning of our end, was when I told you
You don't make me feel wanted

57

you responded
"I don't know what to tell you"

And I just remember thinking
If I have to teach you how to want me
You don't actually want me
Or are you just filling in blank spaces?

Never thought you would make me feel mismatch jigsaw
puzzled
Thought my sharp and misshapen edges are what you fell in
love with
In the first place

Were you ever in love with me at all?
Not loved me, but
Inside of this battle for breath and bravery with me
I was always designing battle plans for loving you better

But I usually feel like I'm fighting by myself
We never question ourselves at the beginning
Because it rarely starts the way it almost always ends
Maybe that's because it usually starts with
"Hi, where did you get that smile from? It looks gorgeous on
you."

Growing

Open Prayer to God III

I have started to question
Started to wonder if you are real
If you are, why haven't I felt you in a while?

So, I'm not sure who I'm praying to anymore
But I guess that's faith

You said I was a good thing
Fearfully and wonderfully made
But are you sure?

I feel like a busy intersection
Like I should come with warning signs and stop lights

First of all, I want to thank you for giving me so much to write about
What is a poet without a tragedy?

Why do you keep taking things from me?
I'm still waiting
I have been praying to you for a while now
I keep trying to stitch all this broken into something that will keep me
warm
My failure is starting to look like a quit ever panel, a picture of an
almost happy ending

Lies | Truths

This is the part where I am supposed to tell you about my happily ever after, but it never evered

So instead, I will give you a list of truths and lies about the last time I was in love

Truth: I'm no longer in love with her

    Lie: I no longer love her

Truth: The nape of her neck is an ocean I wish to drown in once more

    Lie: She loved to touch me, to prune the darkness from my eye and to use her lips to photosynthesize my soul

Truth: I was right to break up with you

    Lie: I'm happy about us not being together

Truth: Others have touched me since she last did

    Lie: Others have touched me since the last time she did

The landscape of this non-relationship keeps shifting, I can feel the atoms turning inside my shifting continents

Lie: I don't want you back

Truth: It will probably end the same way

Lie: I don't care about tomorrow

Truth: Endings are overrated

If you give me another chance, I promise to try and make sure
                we
                   never
                      have
                         another

                          .

                          .

                        .

                   Just leap with
                      Me
                    Once
                    More

Inherited

Things my father never told me
Or warnings I will give my children:
If you are my child, and from what I'm told you most definitely
are
You will have an uncanny ability to spend money you don't
have.... yet
You will want to argue with internet trolls... don't
You are the moon, you are not about barking back at dogs

In college, one of your friends will name you, "puppet boy"
Never deciphered if it was because I was Geppetto or Pinocchio
Either way, you will grow tired of feeling every action has
strings attached

No matter how many layers of clothing a woman has on
you will have the ability to make them feel naked, unprotected
Do not use their vulnerabilities as vantage points
Do not add to the reason they felt the need to wear
so much protection in the first place

You are predisposed to being a
gambling addicted kleptomaniac
Always rolling the dice
with hearts you stole
from people who trusted you

You will fear things and humans you don't understand
but that doesn't mean you should love them any less
You have not been endowed with a spirit of fear
but of power, love and a sound mind, you have a sound mind.

You have a sound mind, but
You will say things that will be perceived

as homophobic, misogynistic, and or just plain offensive
You don't get to decide how your words land
So runway them with a care
Your flight pattern shouldn't
mayday anyone else out of the sky

Don't make excuses
Apologize and mean it
Hurting others is not ok

You're not all bad
Most days
You will make your body a fortress
with a bank vault heart
You will let people withdraw from you
without ever making a deposit
Don't keep track of their account balances
you will be happier this way

PLEASE! DO! NOT! Become a writer or poet
Writers and pain seem to be star crossed lovers
I pray you never have the kind of hurt
That you can draw from an ink well
Poets spend far too much time
falling in love with everything
But themselves

Which is to say, your father is made of heartbreak
Unfinished poetry and
chipped cinder blocks
that wishes itself to be more
cloud than concrete

Translation: I wish I was allowed to be gentle
in public, so that I didn't have to be so hard always

but on the upside this concrete love will make
you sturdy enough to build on

Anger will more than likely be your cornerstone
Do not be afraid to rebuild using only love as a foundation
Do not be the reason you are afraid to love

Be more than broken promises and Monday mornings
On days where your bedroom
feels like a funeral parlor remind yourself
you can die after you have
done all the living you can

Wear your alive like it's going out of style
Wear it like if you miss a moment you won't get it back
Because you won't

My child, I'm your father
Therefore, required to love you
So, I love you

I mean, lucky for both of us
you're lovable and I like you
but even so I love you

Just know
I love you
I love you
I love you

I keep saying I love you because this world
will make you forget you are worthy of love
So again, I love you

I love you so much
I pray you take after

65

your mother

Dry eyes

Depression is not
a satisfying lover but
it's a faithful one

So be very careful
Not to end up in its bed
It will keep you there

Yesterday my thoughts tried
To seduce me, but they weren't
Sexy, they were awkward

Yesterday I was
In a strange, yet familiar
Place it was a bar

I have not been there
Since I saw you last, since I
Said goodbye to you

That day she was with
Me, made letting go tranquil
Just held on to her

Yesterday she wasn't
Yesterday wasn't tranquil, there
Wasn't anything to hold

I was alone and present
Was absent and surrounded
I didn't feel, just sat

It wasn't a year yet
But an honest occasion
Very appropriate

Your hospital bed
In the middle of a bar
Closed in by laughter

I haven't cried over you
And I don't think I ever will
Just dry-eyed goodbyes

Apollo

Apollo, born of Zeus and Leto
Apollo, the god of music, poetry,
Oracles, archery, medicine, light,
Knowledge, and the sun

How unlike me to think myself a god
But how like me to think myself a god

Every morning, Apollo drags the sun across the sky
Gives light to those in darkness

Ain't it just like me to feel I have to bring the sun with me wherever I
go?
To be continually running from the darkness?
To burn anyone who gets too close, yet
Bow and arrow things from a distance?
To be near or far from me is to be destroyed, there is no difference

I can relate a lot to Apollo
To be born of a creature who thinks himself god and king
Who cracks the sky open with his voice

Zeus who never learned what it
Meant to be faithful
No matter how much of a goddess my mother was
My father would find himself in the bed of mortals
But this will not be a poem about Zeus
He has already taken up enough space

Or about how my name was Horus
Until Europe changed it to something
That fits in their mouths more easily

No this is a poem about me being the god of plague and of healing
But people believing me to be either/or and never both
It is about the complexity of an existence you call mythology

I be the brightest, blackest kind of magic
This poem is about how I found Mount Olympus within myself
It is about how my form and ability is not limited to your perception
It is about my ability to oracle the ending of every relationship before
they begin
Whether I see a future or not, I make excuses, say things like:

How can I stay the night?
Don't you know I am Apollo?
It is my job to bring back the morning

This poem is about the darkness fearing me
And me still running from it
It is about temperance
and moderation
and moderation
and moderation
and moderation

Moderation, in all things, especially moderation
Which is to say, I wish a mother fucker would
Which is to say, I will bring the sun to set on your existence if you test
me

This poem is about how I'm afraid to say what I feel, so I hide in
metaphors
It will be about how I keep saying what it's about so I never have to
say it
This poem is about how confusing ourselves for gods is the most
human then we can do

Random Thoughts II

The comment section is the worst play on earth

You can't have a proverbs 31 woman if you don't create a proverbs 31 environment

Daily struggle: I want to date, find a spouse, and meet new people. BUT I don't want to leave my house. ☺

Write About Now feels like a second home.

TAKE THE DAMN TAILS OF MY SHRIMP!!!

Let one more person tell me Girlfriends ain't in the bible. Neither was an iPhone but you still in a committed relationship with that.

HELL NAH

Sometimes I wonder how I am this sarcastic and still have a job. It's baffling.

Contrary to popular belief love don't always feel good

I make inappropriately dark jokes, it's how I process... sorry in advance

HARRY POTTER SUCKS JK JK. Lmao Erica you should

If you're not willing to be vulnerable you're not ready for a relationship

A. Have you ever shared a bed with a friend you were attracted too?
2.If yes how did that go?

So I'm scared of failing my future children. But also I'm supper excited for the day my wife calls me and I'm like:

"They did what? Put they bad ass on the phone."

Thank god for praying Grandmothers and mothers.

"You don't have to strategize if you only slam nucs"- Ebony Stewart

Write better poems- Amir Safi

I'm super regular.

Anger issues? What anger issues?

If

All this woke shit is nice, but I will slap the dog piss out of you keep playing

WHO YOU WIT!

Superwoman

Everyone thinks Superwoman is this
amazing person, and she is, she is.... NOW

You didn't see her when she was temper
tantrum tossing toddler.
When most children scream, you may
figuratively state that the sound is deafening

But she is actually superwoman
So, the sound is literally deafening
I would try to be strict
I would try grounding
But have you ever tried to
A ground a black woman,
who can actually fly?

Never works out how you think it's going to
Her teachers will tell me she has "behavioral issues" or "ADHD"
But she is just bored Brainiac
And they fear a mind they cannot standardize
The media will try to meteor shower her self-esteem
from a phantom zone, always

They will tell her
She has no more to offer the world
than the way she fills out a pair of brightly colored tights

There will be days when she feels there is
no Fortress of Solitude she can call sanctuary
So, I will sit her down and explain that
Darling, you crash landed on a broken world

When your skin is powered by the sun

and your hair defies gravity, you are
more than most mortals can comprehend

Raising children of color has always felt
like trying to raise super heroes
As a black man, you must be twice
as good for half a comic book

As a black woman, you must be adjacent to perfect
You must Smile. You must never raise your voice
at best, they will stereotype the supper sonic
in your voice, bitter black
at worst, resisting arrest

Society is full of super villains that mask their words
Examples include:

>"If that girl didn't want to die, why didn't she keep her
>mouth shut?"
>"If she wasn't looking for sex, why was she drinking?"
>"Why was she out so late?"
>"Why was her skirt so short?"
>**"IF BLACK GIRLS ARE SO MAGICAL,**
>why are they always complaining about disappearing?"

In a perfect world, I would have sons
I teach not to be villains
But in this world, I fear
I will have daughters I must teach
not to be damsels
But to leap over distress in a single bound

I will erect Justice League to protect my daughters
make this whole DC universe Marvel at the way
I turn Avenger and Hulk smash
anything that threatens my children

73

When raising a woman of steel
you must be an Iron Man

They will use you for incantations
and spells to stifle her strength:

> "You know, you're pretty for a black girl"
> "You're well-spoken for a black girl"
> "You're *insert stereotype* for a black girl"

You think black girl magic is powerful?
You should see the rabbits white supremacy
and casual black misogyny can pull out of a hat

Willy Lynch was a wizarding wonder, taught us
keep the body strong
the mind weak
Keep telling her she is exotic
reminds her she is alien
reminds her she is only beautiful
when mixed with other

I know nothing of being a woman
So I will surround her with a village of Amazons
They will teach her the art of warfare in her womanhood
She will stand on the shoulders
of all the Wonder Women who came before her
Ready to save a world that keeps tugging at her cape

She is just as much God as any boy who thinks himself deity
AND SHE AINT GOT TO SHARE THE NAME SUPER WITH ANY
MAN!

My body

As a qualified mental health professional, I'm trained to spot disorders, illnesses, and abuse, IN EVERYTHING

Based on this, I have come to the conclusion that I'm in an abusive relationship. . . with my body

I keep promising I will do better, and I do, until I'm hungry, again, and salad won't satisfy

In the beginning, we were a cute couple even if an awkward pairing

We used to run and jump and play, my body loved me when I didn't have anything else to love

But hurt people hurt people, so I keep force feeding it things not conducive to a healthy relationship

My body is the definition of a ride or die, it got me through more basketball practices than I can count

Not to mention the brutality of basic training

I think I have just always thought it would always be there

But lately my body has been distant and it's making me think it's seeing other people

It's been making me feel less secure about our relationship.

So, I don't let it out of my sight

I keep telling it how worthless it is

If I beat it down, it won't have the strength to leave

Sometimes, I fear it will leave me with no body

Airfare

The airport is a funny place, not Kevin Hart funny, more
Seinfeld funny.
Did you ever notice they smell like anxiety and sleep
deprivation?
Thousands of people all going to tens of thousands of
destinations.
I sit in my fresh out of basic training uniform, doing my best to
show off all the military bearing I have just recently acquired,
as I watch people embrace their loved ones.
I think, what a blessing it is to display that love without
consequence.
To move with so little effort, so freely.
And then it happened, a concourse's eye fixed on something,
an abundance of corneas are locked in fear.
I think it must be some incomprehensible danger.
To my dismay, all eyes are glazed over with prejudice at the
sight of a young lady in a hijab and, what I assume, is her
husband.
A funny thought invades my mind they should require people to
check their Islamophobia with the rest of the things there's no
room for on flights.
They find a seat near mine, and all eyes are still locked on
them.
And there's me, all boots and American flag fastened to my
shoulder, US Army nested just above my heart, and greeting
them with open palms that say, "Welcome."
I wonder if to be Muslim in America feels like black sheep,
scapegoat, like moving target, like burning cross, like go back
to where you came from.
"Flight 3546 from Columbia, South Carolina to Houston is now
boarding."

To be a minority is to be asked to pay for other's perceptions of your worth, and sometimes the price is more than we can afford.

I get up and extend my hand, it is common for civilians to thank soldiers for their service and for soldiers to thank civilians for their support, say to the man, "Thank you for your sacrifice," the man's mouth is wordless, but his grip says, "Thank you for support."

I Didn't Cry Today

Not when I saw his wife
Not when I saw his children
Not when I realized they didn't understand he wasn't coming back
Not when I saw his mother and brothers and sisters and father
Not when they told me how he put a gun to his head in front of his
wife with his two little girls in the next room

I didn't feel like I had earned tears

I didn't feel like I had done enough to make him feel loved and
worthy
and strong
and soldier
and enough

How do you survive being eaten alive by two wars?
Just to have your home devour you

No, I won't cry...

I almost cried when they did roll call
Major Colley
Major Colley
Major Colley
Major Allen Colley

All present apart from Major Colley, Sir
He is no longer in the land of the living

The rifles cried out
Shed their 21 tears
Finally, I cry
Every tear a salute

A soaking wet exaltation of a life gone too soon

Storm clouds ain't got nothing on a company of soldiers mourning their fallen
It was a flood, or reservoir of sorts
I didn't feel worthy of my own tears today
Next time, I hope I will
I hope there is no next time

2nd Date

After the 2nd date, God said: rise, walk away.
RJ is not the sanctuary you have been in search of

Ok, so I have never felt like a holy place
And I've been rejected before
But God being the reason or rejecter is a new one

She said, God told her I am not the one
She told me she asked why and God answered with silence

So my insecurities made an attempt to fill the quiet with all my wicked
They conjure the conversation God had about me with her
Unfurled all my shortcomings one at a time

God said: he's still back alley brawling with the ghost of his earthly father
He has a temper fashioned for war and you have seen enough battlefields
You will not be the hill his pride dies on

He's got too many scars
He's got a lot of broken
And you weren't made to be his bandage

Daughter of mine, he does not know how to love
To wrap another being in agape
Which is to say, he is a broken promise made flesh

He is a Wednesday afternoon hangover and
You, a Sunday morning worship service
You don't need the hair of this dog clinging to your holy

Each truth feels like a quarry dug in the landscape of my body
And finally, I give in to my insecurities
They reinforce the feeling that
I am not enough

I am always alone
Always a lonely 2am in search of company or a lullaby
Or a boat to keep me from drowning in all this hurt

It is not good for humans to be alone
So why would God condemn me to isolation
I just want to be loved, to be made to feel more man than
monster

Am I a monster?
Just another thing that goes bump in the night?

Ya know, it ain't often I meet a
Woman that makes falling in love look less
Like the cliffhanger in a horror movie

That makes me willing to give of myself freely
There is a difference between changing for someone
And changing because of someone

I thought she was my catalyst
But God told her I was a failed experiment

So, I asked, why won't you let me have a good thing?
And he answered with silence
It was so..............silent
I almost questioned whether he was there

But he was
I felt him wrap me in a melody and whisper
As you are presently constructed

81

You are not the one for anyone
So be still, I am creating you a new heart
I'm not done with you yet

I want to be happy about the version of myself
That is coming, but when my lips part
I say, but I'm alone now.
What do I do in the meantime?

And God in his infinite wisdom answered with...silence

Black Magic

To be self-aware is to be frightened for two reasons,
simultaneously
It is to be terrified of your inadequacies
Yet in awe of your potential
And today I choose to immerse myself in the latter
Today I refused to write a horror story
I will write comedy, I will write love, I will write tears of joy
'Til every page is drowning in elation
I'm equal part an experiment in black magic, struggle and joy
My creators were both saint and scientist
Carnage and comedian
So, I be a laughing tragedy pieced together from hell nahs and
hallelujahs
So, I smile
Yeah, this gap-toothed smile be hymn of praise and exorcism
And my skin be a church bell kind of holy
Loud and hypnotic
Holds a melody that calls saints and sinners to the altar of my
feet
My love is a worship of sorts
It is an appreciation for all this black I have been blessed with
This poem be a compilation of every love poem ever shot out of
my mouth aimed back at myself
In an attempt to prune all the self-hatred
So, I am a black diamond, swimming through a sea of
rhinestones
I wonder how long it took God to find the perfect shade of
ebony to wrap my smile in
When I smile, lights brighten in an attempt to smile back
I am an ocean floor of a man with a symphony of phoenix
wings for legs, short gun mouth and Excalibur tongue that cuts
and slashes through beings unworthy of MY COMPANY
My hands be a temple for light

and fight
and pleasure
and pain
They make a kingdom of anything they touch
Glory is at hand
It is crowed in my palms
Fear will not be exalted here
They say this black boy is arrogance
But it is my way of fighting back
Because they said I wouldn't make it this far
Said I won't graduate high school
So, excuse my self-assuredness
Sometimes my alive be a boastful kind of praise
This is the most truthful kind of self-love
Why are we so frightened by the truth?
This tongue be the double-edged sword where both life and
death rest
And so, I'm always striving to make my mouth birth canal
instead of mausoleum
Any mother will tell you creating life is no easy task
It is an exercise in patience and pain and love and relief
Funny how death and life have similar processes, but such
different end states
I'm not yet at an end state
But several trimesters in the making
Pregnant throat swollen with revelation and expectation
Today, I prepare this birth canal for everything my spirt been
gestating
Today, I choose to feel the pain
To feel the hurt
And at the same time, I choose to be happy
To heal
To forgive myself for feeling in the first place
Today, I take my emotions in my own hands
Today, I am more magic than I was yesterday and nowhere
near as much as I will be tomorrow

I Am | 27/30

I feel like I have to prove myself
I feel like I am not there yet
I feel like I am being doubting me
  feel like I am more to me than this
  feel like I am too alone for my own good
  feel like I am still mapping out happiness
        like I am discovering lost things
        like I am a lost thing
        like I am about to find myself
            I am still searching
            I am having trouble finding
            I am human that way
              Am I familiar to you?
              Am I something you can love?
              Am I a question with an answer?
            I am learning I can answer myself
      Like I am growing into my beautiful
I feel like I am finally getting there

Holding On

When I say I write slam poems, I mean
I write the best poems ever....
Until the judges score them

When I say I am a writer
I mean, I am always attempting to rewrite myself
To give emotions a physical form
To make feelings something tangible that I can hold on to
I'm not good at holding on to things

I write a lot about my dad
How he shows up in all the wrong places
How we were always slipping through his fingers
Not being able to hold on to things runs in my family

I write about my inability to love or be loved
How that makes my body feel like an emptied balloon

I don't write about my anger, because it might scare you
You might run from me
I'm something people often run from
I think they mistake me for a starter pistol
On your mark!
Set!
See look at them, GO!

My anger is not a fire
It is an ocean drowning in itself
It's a lost child in a supermarket
It wants someone to hold its hand

This is the only thing I am good at holding onto
It is the shield I hide behind
It is the vault where I keep all my hurt
I mean, what hurt
Pain doesn't make for polite conversation

Good manners are of the utmost importance

I'm not good at forgiveness
But I'm not sure I want to be
They say forgiveness feels like healing
But I wouldn't need to heal
If you hadn't hurt me in the first place

My bones are brittle, and when broken
Never seem to fuse properly
I mean, my body doesn't know how to hold on to itself
I mean healing is always slipping though my fingers

I'm sorry, poems are supposed to have
Concepts and beginnings and endings

But this is all middle
All unable to grasp anything
All trying to hold on while letting go
All hiding place that no one is looking for

Why is no one looking for me?
I think I want to be found
But I never say that out loud

Never asking to be held
Is easier than being rejected
I've been rejected
I mean, let go

People don't like holding on to me
I wonder if it's because I'm too heavy
Am I dead weight?

I mean, if you live long enough
You will see a lot of death:

Maria, Tyler, Grandma, Grandpa, Nana,

Pawpa, Dad, Cousin Chucky, Aunt Charlotte,
Troy, Cousin Johnathan, my last relationship
My first relationship
EVERY RELATIONSHIP

I watched a man die in front of me at a party once
When the shots went off,
it looked like someone threw a rock into a pond
People were climbing over each other in waves

Sometimes, I feel like the rock that the waves run from
I watch him struggle to keep the light in his eyes
To hold on to his last breath
Is it selfish to want someone to hold on to me like that?

Sometimes I feel like a traveling graveyard
Without the flowers
Do you like flowers?
They hold all that light, and beautiful, and alive,
Like they know they will wilt soon

Well, I think I'm done now
Can you hold on to me now?
I may not hold you back
I'm not good at holding onto things

Photo By: Jamaya Michelle Walker

310brownstreet.com
@310BrownStreet

34878239R00051

Made in the USA
Middletown, DE
02 February 2019